Falling in Love
with
Yourself

A Guide to Becoming a Better You

Published by Bre'Yanna Mitriece Enterprises
©2015, Bre'Yanna Mitriece

ISBN-13-9780692400074
ISBN-10-0692400079

First Edition 2015
First Printing, July 2015
10 9 8 7 6 5 4 3 2 1

Printed in the United States of America

TABLE OF CONTENTS

Dedication

For

The forgotten woman
The motherless and fatherless woman
The lost woman
The hurt woman
The bitter woman
The broken woman
The woman struggling with self-worth
The woman who wants to grow
The woman who desires to be loved

May you finally find the love of God and the love of self,
so, you could finally see the Queen inside of you!

Acknowledgements

I have crossed paths with many people and every one of you have touched my life in some way and for that I say thank you.

To my God, Jesus, thank you for my gift of poetry and writing. Thank you for laying this gift before my face. You have shown me that things happen at the appointed time and within the right season. I am grateful for the wisdom you have put into me at such a young age that I can now share with the world.

"Let your light so shine before men, that they will see your good works and glorify your father which is in heaven" Matthew 5:16

To my beautiful daughters Skye and Taighlor, everything I do is for the benefit of you two. You two are my world and until my last breath I will love you with all my heart. You are my brown queens, and you can do and be anything you want, and I mean anything. I love you forever, and forever you will always be my babies.

To my beautiful mother Alice, where would I be without you? You are one of the best people I know, you are so strong and my role model. You will always be my inspiration. You taught me how to be strong, and to always persevere, you taught me how to believe in God. You are my best friend, my confidante, my biggest supporter, my blessing; whatever I lack you are right there. I hope one day Skye and Taighlor will say the same thing about me. I love you!

To my father Jeffrey, Thank God for you. You have always believed in me and always taught me to do my best. You have laid the foundation for me so all I have to do is to continue to build upon it. You are my best friend. You have given me some of life's best advice and that in itself is priceless. I am blessed to have a father that always encouraged me to read and to seek knowledge. I love you!

To my brothers Britton and Brandon, Thanks for believing in your sister, you guys are my biggest supporters, you ROCK with your sister. I am so glad I can make you guys proud of me. You believe in me, in my work, and want I'm doing, and you want to see me become GREAT. I love you guys forever!

To my family and my closest friends, Thanks for believing in me and my first book of poetry "Imperfect Greatness." Thanks for all the kind words, the encouragement, and the motivation. I will be great, and I will do great thing. Keep believing in me as I believe in myself. I love every one of you!

"Falling In Love with Yourself" was written at a pivotal point in my life when I began to reflect on my past and the times, I felt like I lost myself in other people and maintain identities that were not in alignment with who I truly was. I forgot about Bre'Yanna and made men the center of my world. I've always thought I loved myself, but I didn't every time I disrespected myself when I stayed in and tried to maintain unhealthy relationships. There were things I did and took part in that reflected the kind of love I was giving myself. I compromised my morals and values in some of those situations.

In October of 2014, I decided something must change, I was tired of living that way, I was tired of giving myself away only to be left depleted in the end. I wanted a healthy relationship with myself and with others and I knew it began with how I saw myself and how I loved myself. I started seeking God more than I ever did before and I asked him to come into my heart and show me how to love me like he loves me.

I began to release past hurts, and I went within to heal my soul so I could show up better for myself. I wanted more for than what I was settling for. I honored and respected myself. I knew I deserved the very best and gave that to myself and I learned how to be the source of my own happiness. I learned how to be happy alone, I learned how to live for God and myself and I saw the Queen, I always was supposed to be.

I started jotting down notes and quotes and using the wisdom God bestowed upon me and it dawned on me that, I can't possibly be the only woman that has turned her back on herself in search of love and happiness. I found the best part of myself when I started to love me, and I want to inspire you and other women to get back to loving you. Because when you really love you, I mean really love all of you, you will require the very best for yourself in every area of yourself. I wrote this book as a part of my healing and growth but also for you so you can grow to love and become a better you. I fell back in love with myself, and it feels so good. Are you ready to fall back in love with **you?**

Love Always,
Bre'Yanna

What is Self-Love?

I know you've heard the term "Self-love", and you know it's something you need to do but you don't really know how to love yourself.

Everyone keeps telling you to love yourself and you desperately want to scream back,

"How do I love myself. What steps do I take and what does it look and feel like?

When I began my journey, I didn't know exactly what it looked like or felt like, but I knew I needed to treat myself better. How I began to truly know myself and love myself was when I took a journey within and started healing. As I began to heal, I began to know self-love and my life changed.

So, what is self-love?

It's simply LOVE for oneself.

Love can be defined as:

An energy that evokes spiritual growth that encompasses respect, honor, patience, commitment, affection, appreciation, acceptance, trust, and nurture.

When we put SELF in front of LOVE, we are stating where the energy of Love is flowing.

- Self-love is the full acceptance of who you are at the core. The you that honors, nurtures, and respects yourself.

- Self-love is maintaining your own identity and not taking on different persona because your family and or friends or society says you should be that type of person

- Self-love is a journey of unlearning and learning. It is a journey of self-awareness and healing. Self-love is not about perfection but a constant journey of progression.

- Self-love isn't something you find, it's already within, you simply tap into it.

- Self-love is prioritizing your spiritual, mental, emotional, and physical health. Taking care of your overall well-being.

- Self-love is self-awareness, being aware of your emotions, character, desires, and motives

- Self-Love is trusting yourself, honoring yourself and your boundaries

- Self-love is accepting your physical beauty and validating yourself

- Self-love is allowing yourself to make mistakes, learning from them and growing

- Self-love is caring for yourself daily, making yourself a priority in your life

- Self-love is important because when you love yourself, you are motivated to make healthier choices in life, that benefit your overall well-being

- Self-love is important because it allows you to create healthier relationships with those around you

- Self-love is important because it allows you to live in freedom, authenticity, and purpose to live the life you were destined to live.

- To fully encompass self-love, you must be willing to journey within

"You don't need to be perfect to love yourself, all you need is the willingness to choose to love and honor yourself above it all"
-Bre'Yanna

Part I

The Journey Within

The journey within is extremely important to cultivate true self-love and self-awareness

The Journey Inward is essentially looking in the "mirror" at yourself, but going beyond the surface and digging deep

You journey inward:
- To Reconnect with your divine spirit and soul
- To discover who you are
- To cultivate a spiritual relationship with God
- To uncover and embody self-love
- To heal and unpack past trauma and pain to let go unhealthy behaviors
- To rebuild your self-esteem and confidence

The journey within is you essentially coming back home to who you are at your core, you connect with your soul and discover your authenticity and what makes you special.

Chapter 1
The Journey Within

"Cultivating a Spiritual Relationship"

A spiritual relationship with God is extremely important.

It is important because:
- You are a spiritual being having an earthly experience, so you need to be connected to the Source of your being
- God loves you intentionally
- When you grow and mature spiritually it transcends every area of your life
- Your relationship with your God strengthens the love you have for yourself
- Your relationship with God strengthens the love you have for others
- You gain wisdom, revelation, and discernment

To strengthen your relationship with God:

- Make your spirituality a priority by making time to pray and or meditate daily

  You can start by just praying and or meditating 5 minutes a day and as your relationship grows, you can begin to spend more time as you see fit

- Read Spiritual books, Devotionals are also good

Chapter 2
The Journey Within

"Healing the Soul"

Healing means to Cleanse the soul of anything that doesn't produce love. Healing isn't about eliminating your humanity but about coming into Wholeness.

As you begin to heal your soul, it sparks something within that makes you want to care for yourself in a new way. Therefore, it is imperative that you look within to remove the weight of past pain and trauma and tap into self-awareness to uncover the self-love that you've suppressed over the years and bring it to the light.
Healing isn't always pretty, and it isn't linear, it may feel like a roller coaster at times but it is necessary so you can usher in wholeness. Cry if you must. Be patient with yourself! Offer yourself Grace and Compassion!

Healing is a Journey!

To grow into a healthy being who operates in self-love you must release the grudges, bitterness, rage, hate, anger, shame, guilt, resentment and unforgiveness etc.

You can work through these things by following the **H.E.A.L** Acronym

H: Help Yourself
E: Examine Yourself
A: Accountability and Forgiveness
L: Love yourself and Learn

H: Help Yourself

You help yourself by taking the first step and making the commitment and the decision that you want to get healthy.

E: Examine Yourself

This is the mirror work, examine yourself beyond the surface and dig deep where the pain and or trauma you're holding on to lies and begin to resolve and release the pain. This is where a lot of unlearning and re-learning takes place.

Here are some questions that I had to reflect upon, that may help you as you start examining yourself.

What past pain and trauma am I holding onto?

Where am I hurting?

Who has hurt me? Who have I hurt?

What unhealthy behaviors do I display that show up because of the pain I've experience or my conditioning?

Why am I the way I am?

Examining yourself isn't a one-time thing, sit with yourself and do the work to release the pain, although it won't feel good, remind yourself that it's necessary for you to be emotionally healthy. Do this until the heaviness from pain/trauma is lifted and you can finally exhale.

A: Accountability and Forgiveness

Accountability requires you to take responsibility and ownership for the choices you've made that were against your best interest

When you hold yourself accountable you no longer point the finger at other people, but you look at yourself, so you can begin to make wise decisions that are for your betterment

Accountability is not about condemnation; you don't beat yourself down

Example of Healthy Accountability:

Don't say: You're so stupid for staying, you're so dumb for taking him back after he cheated.

Say: I own my part in that relationship, I stayed way to long because I believed we were in love, I do see how I ignored several signs and allowed him to mistreat me and made decisions that didn't benefit me, going for I want to honor myself, my boundaries and make wise decisions that benefit me

Forgiveness is finding peace after the pain and not allowing that pain to live in your present or future.

Forgiveness is for yourself and for others

Forgive yourself for the choices you've made that didn't benefit you

Forgiveness doesn't always come easy, and it isn't an instantaneous decision, it may take time so give yourself that time

Although you have forgiven them that doesn't always mean you have to reconcile

L: Love yourself and Learn

At this point you are uncovering and tapping into self-love because:

1. You decided to get healthy
2. You were willing to examine yourself and feel the pain
3. You took responsibility for your choices
4. You're willing to learn new healthy patterns that benefit you

Choosing yourself and choosing to get healthy is an act of self-love, so continue to cultivate the love within although it may feel foreign at first. It's necessary and needed. It'll become more than a feeling the more you learn and discover who you are, what you like, your passions, your values, the life you want etc. Love becomes who you are.

Healing is your responsibility, but you don't have to heal alone

Additional Resources to assist with healing:

- Journaling
- Therapy
- Mentor

Chapter 3
The Journey Within

"Rebuilding Self-Esteem and Confidence"

What is Self-Esteem?

Self-esteem can be defined as having confidence in one's own worth or ability. To have self-respect for oneself.

Influences on your Self-esteem/Confidence

- Stress from work or at home
- Changes with a spouse, co-worker or a loved one
- No support from friends of family
- Negative thinking
- Societies Standard of living and beauty
- Depression
- Being Motherless or Fatherless

Think about how these influences have made you feel about **YOU.**

Rebuilding YOUR Self-Esteem

Start telling yourself "**I LOVE you!**" daily (even when you don't feel like it)

Start doing things that bring you joy and make you happy. You are the source of your Happiness.

In this chapter, I want to share with you three tips I used to rebuild my self-esteem and confidence.

1. Healthy Affirmations

I stared speaking healthy affirmations over myself. I started with scriptures like, "**I'm more than a conqueror**", "**I'm the head and not the tail**", "**I am the apple of God's eye**" and then I learned the power of "**I AM**' and I began to speak "**I AM**" affirmations over myself. I did this **daily** even when I didn't feel the best.

Healthy affirmations remind you of who you are and what is possible for you. Affirmations are the truth about who you are at the core of your being. When you affirm yourself, you increase your self-esteem and Confidence. Always be conscious of the words you speak about you and about your life. There is power in your words.
I call it "**Speaking Life**". Let your words bring forth life. Let your words pour **LIFE** into you.

Here are a few affirmations to get you started:

I AM SMART AND INTELLIGENT

I AM BEAUTIFUL
I AM LOVABLE AND VALUED
I AM ENOUGH AND WORTHY OF LOVE
     (More affirmations are in the back of the book)

▪ Healthy Mindset

I know you've heard the saying "The mind is a powerful thing" and that's true, it is. Our thoughts about ourselves and our lives shape who we are and what we become.

After doing my healing, I knew I couldn't have an unhealthy mindset if I wanted to produce a healthy life

So, I shifted my thoughts, anytime an unhealthy thought will come, I'll attend to it, and replace it with a healthy thought.

Now, this does take practice, but practice makes better and the more you produce healthier thoughts, you'll feel better and make better decisions allowing you to experience a healthier life.

Remember: Your thoughts are not in control, you are. Change them at any time!

▪ Self-Care

Self-Care can be defined as a daily decision to care for your emotional, mental, and physical health. We care for ourselves mentally, physically, emotionally, financially etc.

Self-Care was instrumental in helping me rebuild my self-esteem. Self-Care allowed me to become the priority. Self-Care reminded me to pour into myself and give the overflow to my family and others

Here are some ways you can Practice Self-Care:
- Treat yourself to dinner and a movie
- Meditation
- Journaling
- Reading a Book
- Saying "No" and honoring your boundaries
- Not attending events that make you feel uncomfortable
- Resting (Doing Nothing)
- Making decisions that are in your best interest even if it upsets someone else
- ....etc

Self-Care isn't only about spending money or etc.

Self-Care is simply about honoring yourself and caring for your mind, body, soul daily.

Bonus Tip: Surround yourself with people who add to your life. Quality people who are healthy are great for your self-esteem and confidence.

CONFIDENCE

Breathe It

With every breath you take Confidence should be exuding from your pores

Your Confidence is rooted in knowing you're no better than anyone but you're not like the rest, you appreciate your individuality

Wear It

Choose clothes that allow you to show up Confidently

When you feel good about yourself, you want to look good as well

Live It

In EVERYTHING you do be CONFIDENT

Live a lifestyle that reflects a confident woman who is secure in God, herself, her relationships, her business and or career.

Chapter 4
The Journey Within

"Defining and Validating Your Beauty"

What is Beauty?

Beauty is a combination of qualities such as shapes, colors or other forms that please our senses.

Erasing America's Definition of Beauty

In America, the definition of beauty has been a skinny fair skinned woman with perfect eyes, a small nose, straight teeth, thin lips, and fine hair.

For many of us, if we didn't look like "her" we were left to feel ugly and unattractive. That definition of beauty was passed down from generation to generation and some of our own parents, family and or friends felt they were unattractive so in return they made us feel like we were unattractive, by not teaching us how to embrace who we are and to love our Skin, our hair, or body shape. Some of us even witnessed it within our own families, the family members that matched societies definition of beauty was often praised and told how beautiful they were and the family member that was the opposite of society's definition was left to feel ugly and unattractive. Those feelings stayed and have been ingrained into some women's mind which has caused some women to seek out extreme measures to become society's standard of beauty.

We must reprogram our thinking and erase that one image of "beauty" that was ingrained into our heads and create our own definition and image of beauty for ourselves. We must understand that ONE image that is being displayed as "beauty" is just ONE definition of beauty and it IS NOT the standard of BEAUTY for all of us. Facing yourself in the mirror and owning your own beauty and rebelling against what society tells you is "beauty" is one of the first steps to erasing America's Definition of beauty and standing in freedom.

Defining Your Own Beauty

My Beauty Story

I was the girl with the big forehead, gap and stretch marks all over her skin. I never knew anything was wrong with my forehead until other people would point out how big it was, and they would make jokes about it. When all your peers have almost perfect teeth, who wants to be the one with the gap, even my brother's gap closed, so why did I still have mine. People would say cruel things about my gap, so I would always smile with my mouth closed and I would laugh covering my mouth. I also used to be really hard on myself about the stretch marks on my skin, I was so afraid to wear my arms out because of those marks on my skin, stretch marks were a "No, No" and considered very unattractive. I mean, why I would want stretch marks and imperfect skin. I wanted to feel beautiful more than anything, I wanted others to look at me and see my beauty. If only they would validate me, I will be able to validate myself. After seeking validation from my peers, I came up short, because I was trying to impress the wrong people. Finally, I had to face myself in the mirror and ask myself "Why do you let other people make you feel bad for what you were born with and the things you had no control over."

At that very moment I realized I was waiting on the wrong people to tell me "I'm beautiful", when I should have been the one to tell myself that all along. I began to dig deep inside, and I taught myself that my beauty was for me to define and validate and if I saw beauty in my forehead and gap then there was beauty in me. I had to believe that there was nothing wrong with the marks on my arm and the elasticity in my skin was something I had no control over. I had to realize that people will always have something to say about how I look, and I can't let that keep me from seeing my own beauty.

I can't control how others feel about my physical features, they have the right not to like them, but I will no longer let other people control how I feel about me. They no longer have that type of power over me. I started to embrace me and my beauty and now I smile showing my gap and I wear my arms out and I don't mind showing my forehead, because I am BEAUTY, I am beautiful, and once I believed it, it became my reality. I refuse to think of myself any less than Beautiful.

<u>Defining Your Own Beauty</u>

Step One: Face Yourself in the Mirror

- Put the naked you in front of the mirror, (no make-up, natural hair, naked)

- Take all of you in

- Most often the only reason we probably dislike some of our features is because of what other people have said about them or because we haven't seen many images representing our type of beauty

- Look at the features you don't like, or the features others made you feel bad about, Start telling yourself those features are beautiful and believe it and own it

- Tell Yourself,

    o Big lips are beautiful
    o Big noses are beautiful
    o Stretch marks are beautiful
    o Flat booty's are beautiful
    o The list goes on.....

- Cry if you must, be real with yourself at this moment

- SAY it and MEAN it (I know it may sound funny talking to yourself, but trust me, you need to be the one lifting yourself up)

- Accept your beauty, you are a masterpiece

- Know that beauty is all opinion based and we all know that everyone has different opinions, so don't take someone's opinion of your beauty, and turn it into a fact

- The Fact is you're beautiful because you've validated and approved your beauty

- Now, I know we all want to be attractive to someone and of course you are. There are millions of people who adore your type of beauty, so if a couple of people don't find you beautiful, don't let them destroy how you feel about you

- You are beautiful and everyone won't think that and that's ok

- When you begin to validate your beauty, you won't crave validation from others. There compliments are like the icing on the cake.

- Physically do what makes you happy with your beauty. Be mindful that you aren't putting yourself or your health at risk or in danger to do so.

- If you are only changing your physical beauty to please other people, reconsider especially if it's something you don't want to do

- Once you start changing yourself to satisfy other people's desires of you, you will always be changing yourself because there will be people who will never be satisfied with your beauty, no matter what you do

- Therefore, you must be Secure in your beauty. You must embrace and appreciate every part of you

Beauty and Make-up and Hair Extensions

- It's perfectly fine to wear make-up, considering you still feel the same way about yourself when you are without it

- You must learn to love your natural hair and utilize the weave, and or the relaxer for convenience, manageability, and versatility

It's best to always love who you are regardless of what's on your face or on your head, your beauty will shine when you have defined your beauty for yourself, and you show up in confidence.

Social Media and Beauty

With social media on the rise and people validating who they are by the amount of likes they receive it is important that you do not allow that to determine how beautiful you are as a person...

- Whether you receive 1000 LIKES or 5 LIKES on your picture you are still beautiful, and I need you to continue to believe that you are

Weight

How much we weigh, and our clothing size plays a huge part in how beautiful we feel

- Love yourself at any size

- If you feel you are at an unhealthy size for your body, set goals, make the commitment, and make the lifestyle changes and get healthy

Part II

Building Healthy Relationships

What is a relationship?

The way in which two or more concepts, objects, or people are connected or the state of being connected

Chapter 5
Building Healthy
Relationships

"With Women"

Building Friendships with Women

I love being friends with women and having that sisterhood because I grew up in a home with two brothers. My one and only sister lived several miles away with our father and was much younger.

I value my friendships with women, I love my sister friends, but I also understand the pain from losing a friend, whether that's because of betrayal, jealousy, being two-faced etc. It can leave an effect on us. There are some women who have never experienced true friendship with other women, and I want you to share in that experience. If necessary be sure to heal from that friendship pain, so that you can open your heart back up to women and building friendship with them.

In this chapter, I want to encourage the building of healthy friendships. Friendships of love, trust, and respect. I want to remind you that women make great friends, and they can be trusted.

To build healthy friendships, you must know and recognize the signs of an Unhealthy Friendship.

Signs of an Unhealthy Platonic Friendship
- Jealousy
- Competition
- Keeping you in drama
- Controlling
- No support
- Take but never give
- Mean

If that list describes any of your friendships. You may want to take inventory of the friendship and see where to place the person in your life and or let them go.

Tips for building Long lasting Healthy Friendships:

- Be a great healthy friend
- Choose and Create a friendship full of support, respect trust and love
- Choose and Create a friendship that practices reciprocity
- Choose and Create a friendship with healthy communication
- Make time for one another when you can
- It's ok to compliment your friend
- Be genuine happy for the success of your friend even when you aren't there yet
- Collaborate with like-minded women
- Motivate, Inspire and Encourage one another

Chapter 6
Building Healthy
Relationships

"With Men"

Signs of an Unhealthy Relationship

To build healthy relationships, you must know and recognize the signs of an Unhealthy Relationship. Although "love" may be present in the relationship that doesn't mean it's healthy.

Here a few Reasons why a woman may find herself in an unhealthy relationship:

- Their definition of "love" is tied to dysfunction, pain, and toxicity
- Lack of self-love and low self-esteem
- Unhealed trauma from childhood or adulthood
- Sex
- They too are unhealthy
- The History or Years
- Fear
- Children

What was your reason for staying in those unhealthy relationships?

Signs of an Unhealthy Relationship

- There's no GROWTH emotionally, financially, spiritually
- Physical, mental/emotional abuse of any kind by him or from you
- Constant cheating and affairs with other women, fighting over your mate, or you're constantly cheating
- Keeping you from God
- You find yourself always compromising and sacrificing your self-worth, morals, and values
- They want to control you and isolate you from family and friends or you are controlling
- You want to end your life or that person's life

- Your self-esteem is low

If you are in a relationship at this moment and you can identify with any of those signs on the list, maybe it's time you move forward.

I've been there and I know one of the hardest things to do is to let go of someone you "love". The thought of them not being in your life, plague your mind and you never really wanted it to end. You hope things would get better, but they never do, and you're left with no choice but to choose what's best for you.

Learn to let go and Move Forward using the **D.E.T.O.X** acronym

D: Delete and Dig Deep
E: Express Your Emotions
T: Time: Take Time Alone
O: Overcome the Pain
X: Xcel, become a better you

D: Delete and Dig Deep

Remove them from your life, by deleting their number and cutting off contact with them. If you have to you can also block them on social media

Take this time to dig deep and reflect on the relationship and why you choose that relationship

Examine yourself and look for areas of growth

Be Accountable to Yourself

E: Express Your Emotions

Know that your feelings are not a light switch

Know that although you're moving on, your feelings may remain

Express any emotions you may feel around this relationship, in your journal, to a trusted friend, therapist and or mentor.

Don't act unbothered if you're not, if your feelings are hurt, that's ok. Feel so you can heal.

T: Time: Take Time Alone

Give yourself time to grieve the relationship, no matter how unhealthy it was

During this time, you can do a **Man Fast(optional)** (30days,90days,3mths,6mths1yr)

You choose however long you want to do this Fast, this is for you to give yourself some undivided attention to heal, reflect and grow

Use this time to explore your hobbies, to date yourself, to go back to school, to start a business,travel, spend time with friends etc.

O: Overcome the Pain

Face the Pain head on, Feel your feelings so you can heal your soul

You know you've overcame the pain:
- When you're willing to open your heart again to love
- You know that there are healthy men capable of loving you

X: Xcel, become a better you

Continue Growing,

Set standards and boundaries for yourself

Be sure to honor and love yourself always

Get out and start dating and cultivating healthy relationship

Bonus Tip: Don't think you have to be at this "perfect healed" place before you can date and or build a healthy relationship. All you need is an awareness of self, accountability and some self-love and healing and you have the capacity to build and sustain healthy relationships.

For my single women who are actively dating.

Tips for a Healthy dating experience:

- Walk in Wisdom, Discernment, and Intelligence
- Go out to connect with people who are for you
- Those who show they aren't for you, let them go or they may become great people to network with
- Honor yourself and your boundaries
- Know that every man you meet/date may not be your "forever"
- Enjoy each moment without focusing on the outcome
- Understand that "Rejection" is a part of dating and has nothing to do with your worth
- Have an open heart, love yourself
- Continue to have a life of your own

- Keep your options open until a man has earned your commitment (You're Single until you're not)
- Be your authentic self
- Ask meaningful questions (marriage, goals, children, values etc.)

  Example: At what age, do you see yourself being married?

  What goals have you accomplished in the last 5 years?

- Be patient and trust the process
- Date your way

  Go out on dates that you enjoy or are open to, don't date based upon society standards. If you don't like fancy dinners but prefer hiking or bowling etc, do that and if you're the opposite and prefer fancy dinners and etc, do that. If you like doing a mix of both, do that. Do what feels good for you

- Don't play games or hard to get, just be yourself
- Always Advocate for yourself
- Make decisions that are always in your best interest
- Honor your standards, lower expectations
- Most importantly, Have fun

Tips for building a Healthy Relationship:

- Show up in your authenticity
- Operate in Patience
- Prioritize the relationship, Ouality Time
- Accept the other person as they are
- If you can't accept a person for who they are, let them go
- Choose and create a relationship of freedom, trust, integrity, respect, love, joy, honor, compassion, and peace
- Create a safe environment and hold space for healing and vulnerability
- Communication is Queen and Understanding is King
- Allow yourself to see reality from your partner's point of view
- Choose reciprocal relationships
- Honor each other's feelings
- Your partner is the "Icing on the cake" they elevate, they complement, they add value to your life
- Mature and align emotionally, mentally, financially, and spiritually
- Pick and choose your battles
- Communicate and ask for what you need

- Your partner can fulfill some needs, however there may be needs you have that need to be met by you and your village
- Have standards, lower expectations
- Have sex often
- Foster intimacy outside of sex
- There is emotional, spiritual, and intellectual intimacy
- Encourage, Inspire, Motivate, Support one another
- Have fun and enjoy life together
- Have your own hobbies and or goals
- Commit to the vision of the relationship
- Utilize therapy and or wise counsel not just when things may be tough but at any time you need support
- Be in alignment with one another and the lifestyle you two want to live
- Maintain your own Friendships
- Don't seek perfection, but progression
- Appreciate and gratitude always, your mate isn't your slave
- Practice Empathy
- You may be triggered, you that as an opportunity for healing

I remember what it felt like to not love myself and therefore this book and sharing my story with you matters because I want all women to know love and come into an awareness of who they are and know they are worthy of everything they desire. Love yourself like your life depends on it because it does.

My prayer is that this book gives you insight and guides you along your journey as you dig deep to transform from the inside out. After reading this book, and putting the information into practice, you will love yourself and experience a HEALTHY, HAPPY and WHOLE life.

I'm going to Leave you with my poem "Queen"

With Love,

Bre'Yanna

Queen©

I'm a Queen, so please bring your best
Mediocrity isn't my thing and I refuse to settle for
anything less
Because as your Queen
I'll be your blessing
No, I'm not cocky, I'm just confident in who I am alone
So, when you come along, know that you'll be adding
to the happiness that I've already found
And what's more profound
Is having a woman on your side whose most priceless
treasure isn't found between here thighs but it's the
knowledge she holds inside her mind
Yea, I can cook, and I can clean
And I can help you write visions to secure your dreams
I'm a Queen, and on this throne, I sit beside you king
Build you up, introduce you to your things
Let you know I'm a part of this team
I naturally submit because you're equipped to lead
I'm a Queen
You can see the essence in the way that I walk
Speak Greatness into you, in the way that I talk
No better than anyone but I'm not like the rest
Come grow with me and she how much more your life
has been blessed
They say "he that found, a wife" has found a good
thing
Well in me you've found your good thing, I'm your
partner, your Queen

Self-Love/Confidence Affirmations

- ❑ I am healthy, happy, and whole
- ❑ I am kind to myself, and I honor myself
- ❑ My life is beautiful, and I will not require it to be perfect
- ❑ I am confident in my strengths, and I grow in my weakness
- ❑ I trust myself and, in my ability, to make wise decisions
- ❑ I am deserving of all that I desire
- ❑ I have a mindset of abundance
- ❑ I will keep my head and self-esteem high
- ❑ Self-love is necessary for living my best life
- ❑ I will always pour from a full cup
- ❑ My mind is healthy and brilliant
- ❑ I make time to nourish my spirit, soul, mind
- ❑ I accept myself for who I am, evolving and getting better each day
- ❑ I give myself permission to be vulnerable, naked, and free
- ❑ I am the best at what I do
- ❑ I choose to be happy
- ❑ Peace and Confidence, Success and Harmony belongs to me
- ❑ I am love, therefore it's present and with me very where I go and in everything I touch
- ❑ I ask for what I want and need with boldness and confidence, and I remain open to receive it
- ❑ I live in my authenticity and my truth

Beauty Affirmations

- ❏ I am beauty and I define my beauty for myself
- ❏ My body is healthy, and I nourish my body daily with exercise and healthy eating
- ❏ I validate myself daily
- ❏ My outer beauty compliments my inner beauty
- ❏ I accept my beauty
- ❏ I accept my hair
- ❏ I accept my skin color
- ❏ I accept my body
- ❏ My body moves beautifully
- ❏ My body is strong
- ❏ My beauty is special
- ❏ Accepting my beauty allows me to be free
- ❏ I release all past beliefs about my beauty
- ❏ Beauty is mine, I am the definition
- ❏ My opinion of my beauty is the only opinion I accept and receive

Healthy Relationship Affirmations

- ❑ Healthy love or nothing at all
- ❑ I will be treated with love and respect
- ❑ I only participate in relationships that are in alignment with my soul
- ❑ I am a magnet for healthy relationships
- ❑ I am open to receiving healthy love
- ❑ My relationships are a place for growth, healing, and love
- ❑ My relationships edify me as I edify my relationships
- ❑ My relationships are safe
- ❑ My relationships give me the space to be my authentic self
- ❑ My relationships are Free
- ❑ My relationships are full or progression and evolution
- ❑ My relationship enhances my self-esteem and confidence
- ❑ My relationships add value
- ❑ I am in thriving relationships that allow me to show up my best self
- ❑ I am honest and trustworthy in my relationships and others
- ❑ My relationships are full of integrity, trust, and honesty
- ❑ My relationships are reciprocal
- ❑ I am in relationships where love is present
- ❑ I engage in relationships with others who love themselves

❏ My relationships are successful and abundantly blessed

For More Resources:

Visit Breyannamitriece.com

www.ingramcontent.com/pod-product-compliance
Lightning Source LLC
Chambersburg PA
CBHW071242090426
42736CB00014B/3190